john cage
uncaged
is still cagey

john cage
uncaged
is still cagey

david
antin

Singing Horse Press 2005

john cage uncaged is still cagey © David Antin 2005

ISBN 0-935162-33-X
Singing Horse Press
3941 Gaffney Court
San Diego, CA 92130

Singing Horse Press titles are available directly from the publisher at www.singinghorsepress.com or from Small Press Distribution (800) 869-7553 or www.spdbooks.org

Contents

Start Making Sense

Back in the early 90s, I was working in my studio on New York's Houston St. with the window open. In those days, people were still playing music on the streets from oversized ghetto blasters balanced on their shoulders and, more often than not, playing hip hop. From outside the window came an array of sheer white noise, which quickly morphed into what sounded like the electronic whooshes of *musique concrète*. I was stunned and rushed over to see what was going on. But by the time I got there, the noise had changed again, this time into light Daisy Age beats. It took me a few minutes to realize that what I was hearing was a noisy break in what was a rare and unique moment for experimental hip hop; a moment that passed quickly once gangsta rap took over. My response to that situation never would have happened had it not been for John Cage and his book, *Silence*, in particular.

Silence was a book I'd long known about. I recall having picked it up in art school back in the early 80s, flipping through it, and rather quickly dismissing it. I had more pressing things to do then, like listen to Flipper, the Dead Kennedys, or bands on the emerging SST label. *Silence* seemed like something from another time: quaint, utopian, oblique; it didn't speak to the times, nor did it compute in the mind of a testosterone-fueled kid in his early 20s.

That all changed a few years later when I hit a wall on the rock 'n roll road. After Minutemen leader D. Boon's death—which I read as some sort of a cultural and personal watershed—I stopped listening to indie rock. This coincided with a bum real estate deal and a career setback, all of which sent me reeling. I'm not sure how it happened, but just when I was at my depths, I was reminded of the cheerful utopianism of *Silence* and quickly sought out a copy. After that, things were never the same.

Like so many generations before me, *Silence* changed everything. It's a book that never seems to go out of style perhaps because its sentiments were never really in style: *Silence* has managed to stay ahead of its time for 40 over years. The interdisciplinary approach of *Silence* opened the floodgates for 1960s experimentation. From Fluxus to Conceptualism, from Judson Church to Happenings, almost every innovative art movement of that decade—be it theatre, music, dance, art or literature—claimed to be driven by *Silence*. Avant-garde vocalist Joan La Barbara sums it up pretty well: "Its initial impact on me was a shock of recognition; its calming effect made me feel that I was not alone in the universe."

Joan once confided to me that audiences were spellbound by John's legendary charm to the point that they would sit through hours of the most forbidding experimentation following his genial introductions. But, she said, the thing they loved most about Cage was the stories he told in works like *Indeterminacy*. Released on Folkways Records in 1959, the piece consists of Cage telling 186 one-minute long stories. The catch is that each story has to last exactly one minute; if a story is long, he's got to speed up to cram it into the time frame; if it's short, he's got to slow down. The constraint gives the piece both its rhythm and its timbre. All the while David Tudor squeaks and honks away on electronics, scored according to chance, occasionally obliterating John's narrative. But as good as the idea of indeterminacy sounds, what really hooks us in the piece is the narrativity of the stories. And this is the great secret about John Cage: we are as intrigued by the myth—the autobiographical elements and the hundreds of tales he told again and again—as by the actual music itself.

This goes for *Silence* as well: for an avant-garde writer, there's nary a page in the book that doesn't make perfect sense; it's eminently readable.

Readable? Listenable? The avant-garde as entertainment?! I think it's something that David Antin's been on to for decades. I've never read anything by David Antin that didn't make perfect logical sense. But it hasn't always served him well. I can imagine in the heyday of the Language poetry moment, with its emphasis on radical fragmentation and subsequent readerly reconstruction, he probably felt somewhat shunned. And in 1972, after Robert Grenier made his now-dated statement "I HATE SPEECH," I'll bet David must have felt like crawling into a hole.

There's a fascinating account of a talk piece that David gave at 80 Langton Street in San Francisco on May 13, 1978[1]. The audience was chockfull of West Coast Language Poets including Ron Silliman, Bob Perelman, Tom Mandel. As soon as Antin launched into a talk about speech and figures of thought, he was immediately interrupted by the hostile audience who began dissecting the structural elements of the piece as they were happening in terms of how they related to the power structures present in the room. Antin, however, took a broader view of things: he seemed to be more interested in the formal aspects of speech and how they related to any given socio-political situation. And as his talk wore on, he discussed the Greek theory of "harmony in speech," a dynamic that occurs when many people are engaged in conversation. What he was doing was not only articulating philosophical theory, but embodying that theory in his performative practice and showing it by example on the spot.

But there was another message in Antin's piece that was as much the medium as it was about the content: present were several tape-recorders. "There were at least six [tape] recorders on a table in the performance area, and their owners were adjusting tapes."[2] While we know that Antin frequently tape-records his performances for later transcription into talk-pieces for the page, it's not clear why there were so many other recorders present, nor was it clear to whom they belonged. But it reminded me of Andy Warhol who wrote about this phenomenon in the late 1960s:

Everyone, absolutely everyone, was tape-recording everyone else. Machinery had already taken over people's sex lives--dildos and all kinds of vibrators--and now it was taking over their social lives, too, with tape recorders and Polaroids. The running joke between Brigid and me was that all our phone calls started with whoever'd been called by the other saying, "Hello, wait a minute," and running to plug in and hook up. I'd provoke any kind of hysteria I could think of on the phone just to get myself a good tape. Since I wasn't going out much and was home a lot on the mornings and evenings, I put in a lot of time on the phone gossiping and making trouble and getting ideas from people and trying to figure out what was happening--and taping it all. The trouble was, it took so long to get a tape transcribed, even when you had somebody working at it full-time. In those days even the typists were making their own tapes—as I said everybody was into it.[3]

Antin's transcriptions of his own speech couldn't be further from Warhol's novel *A*, which was full of spelling errors, inaudible words and vast blank spaces due to the typists inability to make out what the protagonists were saying. David's texts by contrast, are pristine, chiseled constructions whose source was once messy speech. But the texts do have something very important in common. As Craig Dworkin remarks about Warhol's *A*, "So with little in the way of any discernable narrative, and nothing that resembles a plot, the activity of the book's own construction begins to take center stage."[4] Antin's New Langton performance, too, revealed and critiqued its own construction.

It's all about structure. And so are the pieces in this book. While the first piece focuses on the structure of Cage's *Silence*, the second piece entitled, "some more thoughts about structure," takes Cage's performance "Lecture on the Weather" as its jumping off point. David describes the performance as having taken place in a room with open French doors. Just as Cage gets going, the perfect storm rolls in to the composer's delight. Cage always said that he wanted his music to be as unpredictable and as nuanced as the weather. Antin, on the other hand, uses the weather to examine the structural workings of his mind, his moods, his life and his culture:

> crepuscular things dont get to me i look out at the
>   sunset and i measure the degree of pollution by how
> terrifically beautiful it is   the more brilliant it is the
> more polluted the atmosphere . . .

This statement brings to mind Andy Warhol's 1967 film *Sunset*, in which a perfect California sunset is filmed. From start to finish it's one giant cliché. The climax of the movie is when an airplane blasts across the screen, a moment akin to the Empire State Building's night lights being turned on during *Empire*. Unlike the more pure impulses of Cage, for both Warhol and Antin, nature's most interesting state is when it's mediated by culture.

So while this book springs from John Cage, in the end it's really Antin's rebuttal to Cage. In the first lecture, Antin describes his break with Cagean purity as David Tudor witnesses a live performance by Antin:

> . . . i would occasionally catch a glimpse of david
>   tudors face in the audience   because he was looking
> more and more baffled as to what all this perfectly
> intelligible ordinary talking had to do with poetry
> or art   at least within the well defined modernist
> ideas of poetry or art   because it seemed to operate

under no formulaic constraints   it displayed no
   conspicuous formal devices   it worked against no
   arbitrary mechanisms   and in short dispensed with
nearly all the features of the kind of work that david
   tudor   has devoted his brilliant career to interpreting
the kind of work that required the character that ive
   always admired him for . . .

And it's exactly this rejection of Cage that makes Antin's work so relevant to today's cultural climate. But it's a double edged sword: on one hand, Antin's work predicts the widespread success of reality television and anticipates our cultural fascination with someone like Ozzy Osbourne, whose television presence is the most engagingly constructed tedium that has ever existed. We can't take our eyes off the guy, stumbling through the dullness of his own life; we hang on his every slurred word.

On the other hand, David Antin comes from a long line of linguistic reformers who turn our attention to the glories of speech as sprung from the palate. From Gertrude Stein and Ezra Pound, passing through O'Hara and Ginsberg, and continuing with recent probing explorations of normative speech by the likes of Grandmaster Flash or Missy Eliott, Antin has played a major role in what Cage, writing in *Silence*, refers to as an awakening of the senses. "Music is all around us," he says. "If only we had ears." In the ensuing decades, we've acquired the ears; David Antin now supplies us with the hearing aid.

Kenneth Goldsmith
June, 2005
New York City

Notes

[1] Ellen Zweig, "Where Is The Piece: An Account of a Talk by David Antin," in *The Poetry Reading*, ed. Stephen Vincent and Ellen Zweig (San Francisco: Momo's Press, 1981), pp. 174-186

[2] Ibid., p. 181.

[3] Andy Warhol, *POPism: The Warhol '60s* (New York and London: Harcourt Brace Jovanovich, 1980), p. 291.

[4] Craig Dworkin, " Whereof One Cannot Speak," (Unpublished: 2005)

john cage
uncaged
is still cagey

a number of years ago i got a phone call from a singer
named marilyn boyd de reggi about a festival she was
organizing at the strathmore center in maryland to
honor john cage during his seventy-seventh year and
since i was on record as having been an admirer of johns
poetry and music since the early '60s she wanted to
know if id be willing to be on a panel dealing with his
work and give a talk on his poetry   musicians singers
dancers and poets would be coming from all around the
country to realize dozens of his works and perform related
works of their own   lots of my friends were going to be
there jackson maclow marjorie perloff joan retallack
and john himself was going to present a performance of his
"lecture on the weather"

i. john cage uncaged is still cagey

when i received this invitation to come talk about johns
work   i felt it was time for me to come and do it   many times
i was invited to similar occasions   but you know how these
things work out   youre on your way to paris and somebody is
having a gathering in bloomington   and its not possible   or
youre on your way to bloomington and somebodys having a
gathering in paris   so it seems i never found the   right
occasion or it never found me   yet if theres one writer   or
poet to whose work i have responded more profoundly than to
johns   i dont know who that is   and this may seem very
strange to people who know my work   though perhaps not
so strange to people who have known my work for a long time
but it would have sounded strange if i had said this to david
tudor
and as a matter of fact i remember doing a performance
because basically thats what ive been doing lately   ive
been doing performances since nineteen seventy two or three
so lately means something like the last fifteen years
but i was
going to buffalo   to the media study center   where i was
supposed to talk about video art or about narrative   but
whatever i did was going to be a performance engaging
whatever i was concerned with   and i did this performance
and i think stan brakhage and david tudor and robert
creeley all showed up for the performance   and i did this piece
now my pieces are talking pieces   i work out
of a relationship of talking to people   trying to address them
while im exploring something in front of them   actually

maybe talking more for myself than for anyone else   and in
this performance what happened is what often happens in my
pieces   narratives develop   and my thinking moves in various
ways   sometimes somewhat surprising to me   though to
everyone else it sounds very coherent   and seems as though
i had planned it ahead of time instead of following my mind
wherever it wanted to go   at least thats what many people have
told me

    now my way of proceeding seems so very strange to
some people that they find it hard to believe   and this leads to
surprising responses

    i once did a performance in san diego at the end of which
a woman rushed up to me and insisted that she had really
enjoyed my performance even though it made her terribly
nervous   and i was really surprised because i couldnt imagine
anything about this performance that should have made anyone
terribly nervous   so i asked her what made her nervous   and
she said i was afraid that youd forget your lines   and this left me
baffled because i never had any lines to forget

    now in buffalo i was talking in my usual way and getting
more and more amused as i would occasionally catch a glimpse
of david tudors face in the audience   because he was looking
more and more baffled as to what all this perfectly intelligible
ordinary talking had to do with poetry or art   at least within
the well defined modernist ideas of poetry or art   because it
seemed to operate under no formulaic constraints   it displayed
no conspicuous formal devices   it worked against no arbitrary
mechanisms   and in short dispensed with nearly all the features
of the kind of work that david tudor has devoted his brilliant
career to interpreting   the kind of work that required the
character that ive always admired him for

i admire david tudors ability to take spices and herbs that have spilled out of their containers and been mingled together with dried beans and palm sugar and excelsior and a variety of other pieces of detritus of almost equal size and to spend days and days separating them out   and this is a feat that john has celebrated so brilliantly   but its an accomplishment thats not in my character   i dont have the character for hunting mushrooms   im sure i would kill myself on the very first day   if not on the first day   then on the second day i would eat with enthusiasm what i had obviously identified as a perfect edible example of *pluteus cervinus*   it would turn out to be an *enteloma* and id be dead by morning   and i know this about myself   my lack of concern with precise discriminations among beautiful things that have no necessity for me   and my unwillingness to subjugate myself to an arbitrary discipline

so why then would i be the right person to come and talk about john cage   when even in the preface to this book *silence* which i found so meaningful   *silence*   a book i discovered in the early sixties and that was so very meaningful to me   there was something extremely unpromising about some of the attitudes expressed in the preface

but then in the same preface john is also terribly perverse and i share his perversity and admire it   so i suppose that may have made him attractive to me   and then theres the response he makes to a question put to him by m.c. richards   why didnt he one day just give an orthodox lecture because it would shock people more than anything else he could do   "i dont do these lectures to surprise people" john said   "but out of a need for poetry"   that sounded right   i understood it or i thought i understood it   it was a promising attitude   it turned me on and i approved of it   but what followed didnt turn me on at all   because john goes

on to say   "as i see it poetry is not prose simply because poetry
is one way or another formalized   it is not poetry by reason of
its content or ambiguity but by reason of its allowing musical
elements   time and sound   to be introduced into the world
of words   thus traditional information no matter how stuffy
    the sutras and shastras of india for instance was transmitted in
poetry   it was easier to grasp that way"
                                god what a reason
    theres the need for poetry   a defective memory   this is the
reason that eric havelock seems to have proposed for homers
putting those elaborate stories into verse too   people had
defective minds and were unable to remember stories   so they
said things like   "we know what all school children learn
    those to whom evil is done do evil in return"   and that made
these stories much easier to remember   its a funny idea and
probably the only silly idea in eric havelock's great book the
preface to plato   and john goes on to point out that karl shapiro
    a poet of whom i have a very low opinion   karl shapiro may
have been thinking along these lines when he wrote his essay
about rhyme in poetry
        now this certainly raises the question of how john cage
could be a poet i am terribly attracted to
                                but there are other
comments about poetry in john cages work   there are
comments about poetry throughout this book   and there are
comments john makes about music that really seem to be about
poetry   and im not sure that theyre about music at all   but in
music im an educated tourist   thats very important to
remember   i dont make music   i have no desire to make music
    im interested in music the way im interested in paris   i know
my way about paris reasonably well   thats about my
relationship to music   so if you are an educated tourist you

dont have too many profound opinions about paris   and i dont
have too many profound opinions about music   i just let it
happen and take my pleasures as i can   and i can in fact listen
not with equal pleasure   but with equanimity to milton babbit
and john cage
                    just a little while ago somebody mentioned them
in the same sentence   so i will also mention   them in the
same sentence
                    but while im a musical tourist im a sufficiently
educated musical tourist to understand that there is something
about milton babbit that has caused people to call him a
formalist   and at the same time there is something about john
cage   for example that comment about poetry i just referred
to   which would also cause people to call him a formalist   but
i would assert the following two propositions   if milton babbit
is a formalist john cage is not a formalist   and if john cage
is a formalist milton babbitt is not a formalist   this is not a
syllogism but there is something axiomatic about it   and the
reason for it is this   john cage belongs to a class that excludes
milton babbitt from its membership   and milton babbit is a
member of a class that excludes john cage from its membership
this is as simple as a venn diagram   and it seems to me that
its almost self evident   and given this class analysis   i figure
that its only because im a musical tourist that i can listen to both
with equanimity though not with equal pleasure
                    but going back to the other kind of commentary on
poetry that i found in johns writing   theres a comment that
comes up in one of the daniel charles interviews   the third
interview i think   and daniel is obviously getting exasperated
with john   and john is getting a little exasperated with daniel
probably because they were living a long talking life together
and this was getting harder to do as time went on   and in

the course of this interview daniel asks john an odd question
   "does silence as you understand it represent the style of life
you desire"   to which john replies   "its the poetic life"   and
here daniel responds with some exasperation   "why do you
insist on the word poetry"   to which john calmly reponds
   "theres poetry as soon as we realize that we possess nothing"
         now i liked that answer even though i wasnt sure what
it meant   because its not about musical elements or meters or
rhymes   but daniel pushes him further because theyre talking
about silence   cages idea of silence   so daniel asks   why
after having done silence didnt you leave it without a sequel or
always do more of it   and john answers i didnt say that i had
attained to silence
         now this attitude towards poetry is somewhat different
from the one expressed in the notion that poetry is something
you do to prose to make it memorable by introducing musical
elements   after all what could it mean for john cage to
introduce musical elements   whats a musical element   whats
not a musical element for the john cage who asked the question
is the sound of a truck passing outside of a music school
musical   is the sound of a truck passing without the music
school nearby musical   is the image of the truck passing
without the sound of its passing musical   it seems to me i dont
know what john meant in emphasizing the musical elements of
language
         im not sure what the musical elements of language are
   it occurs to me there are many elements of language that we
might consider musical   musical   pitch curves or images or
absences   that we might propose to the mind that might quiet
it   if i may borrow one of johns formulas for what music
brings to the soul
                  i say formulas because theyre catch phrases

that john has either invented or quoted that seem to sum up
succinctly certain ideas and attitudes that he is attached to and
  seems to   carry around like baggage wherever he goes   but
if these are catch phrases hes made them or made them into
  them   hes a man whos invented commonplaces and given
them different meanings each time he uses them again   so that
his repetition is a form of translation   and maybe hes always
  translating his past circumstances into his present circumstances
    which is why he seems not to be repeating himself   and
of course hes not repeating himself any more than homer
is repeating himself with his *topoi* in the odyssey or the iliad
    though johns *topoi* are not contemporary cultural
commonplaces   but the commonplaces of a spiritual tradition
that he is continually adapting to   contemporary living

          but to get back to what i learned from the book i collided
  with   what i learned from *silence* seems to be different from
what most people learned from it   the first piece that really
  astonished me was one of the most brilliant pieces of poetry
i had read in many years   it was the second movement of a
work called *composition as process*   well now there is a question
of whether its one work in three parts or a suite of three works
  whether its one poem or a sequence of three poems with an
epilogue   the work consists of three lectures given in
  darmstadt   and several other places probably   modified by
the way theyre set up in somewhat different typographical forms
    lectures that make more or less didactic statements about the
organization and structure of music as an activity undertaken
    as doing something concrete and particular   that seems to be
whats at stake

          and the first one   which is a historical account of johns
  ways of working   is interesting and reasonable enough   but
it was not the one that most attracted me   part one   the first

movement   if we can call it that   was not what attracted
me   while the third part consists of a series of provocational
questions   that are attractive enough   that is theyre
provocational enough to be attractive to me   but it was the
second part that most moved me   it was this intractably ugly
looking second part   printed in blunt paragraph blocks in very
small type   that john himself decribes as pontifical in character

   what got me first about this piece was its ugliness   it
showed how far you could go into unpromising material and
still come out with a poem   and then there was the physical
difficulty of reading it

   though i had good enough eyes then to read it   but
it took an effort   and then what i liked about it was its
agressiveness   the piece is a calculated act of aggression

   even its typography and layout are acts of aggression   the
piece   if one reads it carefully enough is an assault on
stockhausen with some fairly severe strictures on earle brown

   that is   its a polemic attack on stockhausen and on the
claims made for stockhausen   but what struck me about
this contentious critical piece was that   without agreeing or
disagreeing with its polemical position   what i received from it
was a feeling of such deep aesthetic satisfaction and approval
that i would call the work beautiful

   now on the face of it is hard to say how you could call a
work beautiful that sounds from its beginning like this

> This is a lecture on composition which is indeterminate with respect
> to its performance. The *Klavierstueck XI* by Karlheinz Stockhausen
> is an example. The *Art of the Fugue* by Johann Sebastian Bach is an
> example.

   now is this musical or not   it seems like a strange way to
open a poem   but the whole piece is divided into six sections

stanzas or cantos and each section opens with the same opening
line

This is a lecture on composition which is indeterminate with respect to
its performance.

is this repetition simply a musical device   the refrain
of a rather odd long limbed song   is this a zen master in an
aggressive mood driving home an argument he wont let us
forget   or is there   something parodic about it   something
about this statement that we must regard with skepticism
     its a statement that is made 6 times   and each time   it
seems to hold out to the performers a promise of unimagined
bliss   and the most curious thing about this lecture   aside
from the fact that it is divided into six sections or five sections
and an epilogue   each beginning with the same opening
line and containing irregularly recurring passages   is that it
proceeds by way of comparisons   and a comparison is a binary
relationship of the kind that john specifically rejects as a way of
looking at things
     the first section compares *the art of the fugue* by johann
sebastian bach to *klavierstuck xi* by karlheinz stockhausen   the
second compares morton feldmans *intersection 3* with cages own
music of changes while sections 3 and 4 which deal respectively
with *indices* and *4 systems* by earle brown   are implicitly
compared to section 5   which deals with christian wolffs *duo
II for pianists*   as well as to feldmans *intersection 3* and bachs *art of
the fugue* in sections 1 and 2
     now i also take a dim view of comparisons and im always
surprised by the excellent art historians in my school because
theyre always comparing things   apparently all art historians are
born with two slide projectors   and you might be surprised at
what can be compared by means of them   a wooden shoe and

a gothic cathedral for example though they dont do that   but
ive often wondered why not   because its possible to compare
anything to anything else once theyre in the same place

in fact theres no possibility of denying a relationship
between two things put into the same place   of course you
can say its not a significant relationship   but there they are
these two things occupying adjacent rectangles   which is a
relationship in itself   so you cant help comparing them

in this piece you cant help comparing johann sebastian
bach and karlheinz stockhousen   john cage and morton
feldman   and earle brown and christian wolff   because they
are all in a relationship   and relation is something that john
emphatically denies liking   especially in this piece

and this piece lives on a comparison of the relations of
various composers and their compositions to their performers
and on their ability provide them with sufficient indeterminacy
to allow them to attend to no matter what eventuality   thats the
key term   apparently the most elevated possibility in this poem
which i love and find it funny that i love it   is evoked by this
phrase   "attending to no matter what eventuality"   which
achieves a lyrical intensity that is hard to believe   and by the
end of this poem you realize that what you most desire in life is
the capacity to attend to no matter what eventuality   and you
come to feel deliriously attracted to engaging with no matter
what eventuality   whatever that might be   a flat tire   a
sudden inheritance   a trip to tanganyika   and each
composition discussed in this piece   is examined in terms of its
capacity to permit its performers to respond to no matter what
eventuality as a result of the determinate or indeterminate acts of
its composer

so these determinate or indeterminate acts undertaken by
these composers are examined for their control or lack of

control of the various elements of music   which john specifies
in great detail and goes over several times   "structure"   which
he defines as "the division of the whole into parts"   "method
which is the note-to-note procedure"   "form which is the
expressive content   the morphology of the continuity"   and
the "characteristics of the material"   the frequency duration
timbre and amplitude of the sounds   or silences of which it
consists   and each of these composers is rated for his success
or failure to liberate his performers to attend to no matter what
eventuality

      stockhausens *klavierstueck xi* is compared unfavorably to
bachs *the art of the fugue*   because in *the art of the fugue*   the
structure method and form are all determined   and the
frequency and duration characteristics of the material are also
determined   but since bach didnt specify instrumentation or
provide much in the way of dynamic markings   the timbre
and amplitude characteristics are indeterminate and left to the
performers   and this indeterminacy brings about the
possibility of a unique overtone structure and decibel range
for each performance   so that the function of the performer
according to john   is like that of someone coloring in a coloring
book

      while in stockhausens *klavierstueck xi* all the characteristics
of the material are determined   as is the note-to-note
procedure   the structure   the division of the whole into parts
is also determinate   but the sequence of the parts the form is
indeterminate   which suggests the possibility of a unique
expressive content for each performance   but according
to john   the great promise of *klavierstueck xi* is not fulfilled and
all hope is frustrated because of stockhausen's choice of
the two most conventional aspects of european music   the
twelve tones of the octave for the frequency characteristic of

the material and the regularity of the beat that is a component of
the method   and these   according to john   render the
indeterminacy of form-giving pointless and incapable of bringing
 about any unforeseen situation
           now the whole poem proceeds in this precise way
     feldmans *intersection 3* is seen as liberating its performer
     while johns own *music of changes* is seen as enslaving the
performer   christian wolffs *duo II for pianists* is seen as liberating
its performers   while earle browns *indices* and *4 systems* are seen
 as enslaving their performers
           and in each case the conclusion seems to be based on
 a precise analysis of the way in which the composer sets up
 a situation that either allows or prevents the performer from
encountering a situation sufficiently unforeseen to allow him to
 engage with no matter what eventuality
           now you may or may not agree with this analysis or
 its conclusion   and i personally have grave doubts that the
invocation of a table of random numbers or chance operations
will invariably or even often produce the kind of unforeseen
 outcomes that allow a performer to identify with no matter what
 eventuality
           but this is a poem that provokes you to think very precise
thoughts just to find out whether you agree or disagree with
 any part of it   and this is as much a part of the pleasure of
this poem as its repeated invocations of the deep sleep of indian
mental practice or meister eckharts ground   from the very
 beginning the initial definitions provoke questioning   for as
soon as john didactically   and somewhat pedantically lays out
the elements of music   as soon as he defines structure as the
 division of the whole into parts   i am moved to doubt   and
 as he repeats it over and over again in each section of the poem
   i begin to doubt it even more strongly   it seems to me

about as plausible as wittgensteins proposal that "the world is everything that is the case"

    so reading this poem im moved to ask   what do you mean structure is the division of the whole into parts   so im reading a poem   and i have to think   thats already unusual and the first thing im moved to think is   is this really the case

    if i was to speak of the structure of a gothic cathedral lets say   the first thing i would think about the structure of a gothic cathedral is that it consists of a series of translations the downward vertical thrust the great weight of the vast roof   its downward pressure   is translated by the contrivance of the arch into a lateral pressure   or in large part into a lateral pressure   contained by the walls   or partially contained by the walls   because in the gothic esthetic the walls are thin and perforated by windows to admit the light beloved of the gothic designers   so that the great lateral pressure transmitted from the arch is only partially contained by the walls while the rest is passed on to the buttresses   the heavy vertical piers placed at intervals along the nave and anchored in the ground right alongside the body of the nave   but since the greatest lateral thrust transmitted from the arch is positioned high on the buttress and acts like the force at the end of a lever whose fulcrum is a great distance down in the ground   much of this force is passed on by another translation to the flying buttress which transmits it as yet another arch or an angled vector to a place farther away in the ground

    now looking at this series of translations as the structure of a gothic cathedral is somewhat different from thinking of it simply as the division of the whole into parts   its a division of its constructional whole into functional parts

but maybe this isnt a good enough model to raise the
question of structure   so lets consider the structure of an
airplane   what are its parts   i would say theres a motion
generating system they call it the engine   then theres the
direction giving system which seems to divide into several
separate direction giving systems   a forward directional system
which used to be the propeller and now is the jet system
which governs both forward and backward directions   then
theres the wing   which governs vertical motion   and the
tail assembly   that governs lateral motion   and there is the
landing gear   which enables rolling motion on the ground
and all of these interact with a subsidiary element   the
wingflaps   which determine several kinds of motion
modification   and when you put this all together you may have
the structure of an airplane   but is this what john had in mind
by defining structure as the division of the whole into parts
and is this an adequate account of the structure of johns
music or of this poem
              i know that john is a counting animal and i also like to
count and i know that there are musical pieces of his that are
arranged on the basis of a module of fours   and that four is
easily multiplied to give you 16 or 32 or 64   and that all of
these numbers are powers of 2   and all of these numbers have
pleasant geometric expressions in squares or cubes
              so i looked very carefully at this poem and it didnt look
like that   it might be delightful for it to be arranged that way
it would be playful but im still not sure that would count as its
structure   still i tried to consider it
              johns poem is divided into six sections   and each one is
constructed of a number of paragraphs   but it is an unequal
number of paragraphs   section 1 has 5 paragraphs   section 2
has 4 paragraphs   section 3 has 3 paragraphs   this suggests a

declining series   but section 4 has 6 paragraphs   section 5 has
2 paragraphs   while section 6 has 3 paragraphs   so if there is
an oscillating paragraph series it runs 5 4 3 6 3 2   which so far
doesnt really add up to a series   so i tried to count the lines
    the sections have different numbers of lines   so i counted
the lines   and i found that the first section contained 59 lines
the second 52   the third 32   the fourth 63   the fifth 44
and the sixth 66   and this doesnt tell us much of anything
    numbers like this do not suggest anything we could call a
structure
            so what is the structure of this piece
            there are six sections and each makes use of several
different language genres   there is the language of analysis a
language of description that includes the language of definition
    structure is ...   method is....   form is...   which lays out
the elements deployed in the compositions to be analyzed
    and then theres the language of metaphor that is invoked by
the analysis but works differently   bachs performers function
like children coloring in a coloring book   feldmans performer
is likened to someone given a camera who can take any pictures
or kind of pictures he likes   the conducter in earle browns
indices is compared to a contractor following an architects plan
and the performer to a workman who does what hes told
    while the performer in christian wolffs *duo II for pianists* is
compared to a traveler who has to keep catching trains whose
unpredictable arrivals and departures are just in the process of
being announced   so we have the childlike colorist   the
improvising photographer   the construction worker and the
harried railway traveler   and in the *music of changes* we have the
slave
            but there is also the language of narrative in the account
of the branching paths by which a performer may or may not
arrive at the ground of meister eckhardt

> . . . He may do this in an organized way which may be subjected successfully to analysis. . . . Or he may perform his function . . . in a way which is not consciously organized (and therefore not subject to analysis)—either arbitrarily, feeling his way, following the dictates of his ego; or more or less unknowingly, by going inwards with reference to the structure of his mind to a point in dreams, following, as in automatic writing, the dictates of his subconscious mind; or to a point in the collective unconscious of Jungian psychoanalysis, following the inclinations of the species and doing something of more or less interest to human beings; or to the "deep sleep" of Indian mental practice—the Ground of Meister Eckhart—identifying there with no matter what eventuality. Or he may perform his function . . . arbitrarily, by going outwards with reference to the structure of his mind to the point of sense perception, following his taste; or more or less unknowingly by employing some operation exterior to his mind: tables of random numbers, following the scientific interest in probability; or chance operations . . .

identifying there with no matter what eventuality
         and it is the interaction of these three or perhaps four
language genres that determines how this poem is constructed
         now these language genres may count in cages sense as
the material of the piece   their repeated but free deployment
their expansion and contraction within the different sections
could count as the method   and their precise positioning
might count as the form   the morphology of the continuity
    but i would question whether that alone could determine the
expressive content of this work
         and where does that leave the notion of structure   is it
simply the notion of six sections   five dealing with individual
compositions and a sixth offering some kind of conclusion and a
prophecy   this seems hardly adequate   because the most
  important thing about this piece appears to be left out   the
nature and effect of the ritualized and yet free repetitions of
  the materials   this is particularly marked in the account of
the pathways leading through the deep sleep of indian mental
practice and the ground of meister eckhart to the ultimate
  confrontation with no matter what eventuality   for these

repetitions change this narrative account into something like an
  incantation   as the narrative expands and transforms finally in
the fifth section on christian wolff   to invoke meister eckharts
  adjurations   to the prospective performer who turns away from
himself and his ego-sense of separation from other beings
  and things and faces the ground of meister eckhart   from
  which all impermanencies flow and to which they return   and
is four times adjured that thoughts arise not to be collected and
cherished but to be dropped as though they were void
     thoughts arise not to be collected and cherished but to be
  dropped as though they were rotten wood   thoughts arise not
to be collected and cherished but to be dropped as though they
were pieces of stone   thoughts arise not to be collected and
  cherished but to be dropped as though they were the cold ashes
of a fire long dead
          thinking about this piece   i believe its more useful to
  consider its structure as the organization of its function and ask
how does this piece function   to which i think we can answer
     it functions as an art machine   so what is an art machine
     an art machine is a system whose parts when put in motion
act upon each other in such a way as to cause you to see things
differently   i believe thats a reasonable definition of an art
  machine   and i remember a long time ago teaching a class
with a very large number of students   and asking them as an
  assignment to make an art machine   and because none of the
students appeared to have had any experience of an art machine
  and feeling that no description would be equal to seeing one
     i sent them to look at one
          now this was in the late sixties or early seventies   and
  the town of la jolla which was the closest shopping center to
where we lived   was at that time still inhabiting the nineteen
fifties

respectable women wore white gloves while their men
wore blue blazers with brass buttons and pale slacks   and most
of the clothing stores sold clothing to accommodate their taste

but my wife elly is an artist not a respectable woman and
is also very small   so the only place in la jolla she could shop
was in the junior section of the local saks fifth avenue   where
they sold things like miniskirts and silver courrege boots

now this junior section had a jukebox   and if you were
bored or otherwise so inclined   you could put a quarter in and
hear the rock tunes of the day   and one day i put a quarter in
carefully selecting b3

as i watched   a mechanical hand that had
been resting at the end of a long gantry rose up and traveled the
length of the track along the row of vertically stacked discs and
came to a stop at b3 reached into the rack grasped the disc lifted
it out traveled to where the tone arm and needle were situated
then turned around and traveled back to b3   where it replaced
the disk retraversed the entire rack to its starting place and then
lay down

so i said to my class which had never seen an art machine
and was apparently having a great deal of trouble finding one
i said   there is this device on the second floor of saks fifth
avenue in la jolla that is an art machine   if you go there you
will see a very brilliantly lit machine of many colors   if you put
a quarter into it its lights will flash and itll start to work   its
right near the place where they sell the silver boots   and if you
put your quarter in   youll be expected to make a selection of
very great importance involving a number and a letter   think
carefully before making your choice   then push a number and a
letter   and what you see next will be an art machine in
operation

in the days afterward between meetings i would run into
class members   it was a class with a hundred and fifty kids and
i would run into them in revelle plaza or in the bookstore   and
they would see me and wave and laugh happily   and i was
happy because of the way they looked   and if they came up
to me i would laugh and ask them are you working on your art
machine   and theyd say im hard at work on my art machine
but one kid i ran into looked very glum   and i asked him
are you working on your art machine   he said no   i dont
know how to make one   so i asked him didnt you go to the
second floor of saks fifth avenue and do what i told you   he
said i went to the second floor and i did what you told me but i
never saw any art machine
what did you do i asked
i went up there and i put a quarter in this machine he said
i pushed b3 and it played the shirelles
it must have been broke i said

the strathmore center is housed in a small neo-classical building on lush green grounds   and johns performance of his "lecture on the weather" took place in a small conference room whose french doors were opened into the front atrium because of the size of the audience

while the performance was going on   a storm that had been threatening all day broke out just at the point in the performance where you hear the recording of wind and rain and thunder   and the storm reached its full fury its lightning flashing and thunder roaring outside right as the simulated lightning from the film appeared projected on the screen to johns incredible delight   in the afternoon with the storm gone i did a second piece for john

ii. some more thoughts about structure

        i remember that somewhere john mentioned attending a
   friday night ceremony in a synagogue and being delighted that
   he couldnt tell when anything actually began or ended   and ive
   always had a fondness for that method of beginning   so if
   anyone else wants to walk across the room bringing in a harp in
   a mitten
            when jackson was performing one of the nicest things
   that happened was that what looked like an immense claes
   oldenburg mitten walked into the room and then disrobed to
   reveal itself as a harp   then there was a piece of sheet metal
   coiled into a cylinder that one of the percussionists laid down
   in the corner near the doorway   a woman came through the
   door followed by a little child straggling after   the child took a
   look at the metal coil   bent down to examine it and promptly
   crawled into it
                 and all this was happening while jackson was
   doing his reading   and ive insisted on keeping the doors
   open during my performance   so i guess i rather like these
   indeterminate effects on the structure of my work   which is
   often indeterminate with respect to its audience
            and this brings me back again to a kind of unfinished
   business with structure   theres something about the notion of
   structure that has interested me for a long time   and ive never
   been quite satisfied with my understanding of it   although
   i spent a lot of time revolving it in my mind   and since the
   consideration of structure has emerged as part of my thinking
   about johns poetry and i still dont think ive thought it through
   adequately   i thought i would think about it once again because

thats what i do   think about things   and since this is also
 a performance that is indeterminate with respect to its subject
matter   it occurred to me that i might go back to my dialogue
with john and what i was thinking about structure there   to see
 why i feel unsatisfied by it
          now in thinking about structure the first thing that came
to my mind was something tangible and solid   like a building
    and thats all very well   architects build buildings to be solid
and closed to the elements   though they are usually though
mildly perforated   for light for air   but one thinks of a
 building as something that encloses   shelters   and perhaps
encourages certain forms of activites   if its not a jail
          i can imagine constructing a building as a jail or prison
 but you dont usually think of building a house as a jail and the
question of how to build a house so it wont be a jail but will
nevertheless be a shelter   has a lot to do with what i think about
 structure and its relation to openness and closedness
          my wife and i were thinking of building a house   or
really rebuilding our house to make it more livable   now my
 wife and i are both artists   and the thought of building a
house is a frightening thought   but building a house for two
artists is an even more frightening thought   yet we thought that
 maybe we should build   we thought maybe we should build a
new house or radically rebuild our old one
          we live in southern california on about three acres of
 sagebrush so we call it a sagebrush ranch   and theres a little
house on it that was not built but dragged onto the property
 from some place in san diego where it had served as part of
 the marine barracks   actually there were two houses   and they
put the two houses together in the middle of our sagebrush
 ranch   put them together with a great deal modification and
 success   we were the second or third occupants of the house

a friend of ours had occupied it before and she made
modifications in the earlier house   which had been rather
beautifully planted by the first owner of the house   a japanese
lady with a very subtle sense of vegetation   so the place was
rampant with growing things   for which we deserve very little
credit   except that we maintain them in a casual manner
and they form a kind of central place around the house and a
kind of   perimeter   beyond which there is californias coastal
chapparal   and at the outer edge of our perimeter we have the
obligatory couple of palm trees   because in southern california
everybody has a palm tree as a sort of symbolic committment to
internationalism
                              theres a belief in southern california that all
of california south of santa barbara has strong affinities with
the mediterranean   and this belief is represented by palm trees
while our bedroom window is shaded by bougainvillea
a gorgeous purple flowering bush that connects us to the
lush islands of the south pacific though we are in fact living in a
coastal desert
                    now our bedroom is completely obscured in its
relationship to the outdoors   we have no shades
                                                            not that
anybodys likely to come unannounced onto our property at
inopportune moments anyway   our nearest neighbor lives a
quarter of a mile away   but even if one did he couldnt see
anything through our bedroom window   we cant see anything
through our bedroom window but light   and we see this light
through a kind of purple veil   produced by the profusion
of blossoms cascading over the window growing up the wall
crawling onto the roof and trying to take over the entire house
the bougainvillea has covered the two windows of the
bedroom and the entire wall so that we have to keep the side

door open to get enough air to breathe till colder weather comes
and the blossoms fall and we can close the door again

so we had been somewhat adapted to living in this place
when we decided to build a deck off the western side
of the house   and in a fit of constructive excitement i found
a friend and said lets build a deck   we designed it in intricate
ways not to disturb the canary island palms that had been planted
too close to the house and a young eucalyptus   that was also
too close and had some growing to do   because ellie has a
special relation to trees   she regards trees as people that dont
move or dont move very much   and she figures they have
rights just like anyone else   and destroying a palm tree would
be murder   so naturally we took this for granted and we
designed the deck so that the palm tree would grow up inside
it   we also cut an indentation in the deck to be fitted to the
curve of eucalyptus trunk in such a way that it would still be
fitted to the tree as it increased in girth over the years   because
we had no intention of ever moving from this place   so weve
tried to adapt to the building and keep the building adapted to
the environment

but the building itself   the construction of the building
was accomplished in a way that as a craftsman i find completely
offensive

its true im not a practicing craftsman   but ive had
enough experience building to have absorbed a craftsman
esthetic   and the construction of this building offends me
ive had to repair things and in this building you never know
whats supporting anything   where beams are behind the wall
whether theres underflooring   you cant tell anything till you rip
out the surface   and then youre in for a surprise   it was
designed insanely   but of course it wasnt designed and design
is sometimes a form of entrapment anyway   but our house

wasnt designed it was slapped together   it was two buildings
put together around a fireplace   which sounds very cozy but its
not   its in the living room this big fireplace   and the two
buildings come together right around it   and since the two
buildings have different rooflines this causes great difficulty in
sealing them together   so its hard to keep the water out during
the rainy season   because there is a rainy season in southern
california in spite of the fact that san diego is really a coastal
desert

in fact one of the first serious questions i asked about
structure was about southern california climate   because
when i first got there i didnt have a clue to the changes or lack
of changes in the san diego weather   they made absolutely no
sense to me   i got used to them pretty quickly but i had no
sense of their structural coherence   day after day of sun   day
after day without rain without clouds   nothing would happen
then it would finally all end   though this end would begin
with a subtle change   the morning and evening coastal
overcast would begin to extend further into the day and finally
would cover the whole day

this would happen mostly in june and november   this
overcast is most extreme in june   we arrived in june   and i
always thought of june as one of the most beautiful months of
the year   but not in southern california   on the san diego
coast its a dull grey month before the arrival of summer   when
the sun comes out and stays and stays   till november   and
the rains start to come and the weather gets cold in november or
december   though mostly it rains and we feel the rain on our
sagebrush ranch much more intensely than people living in the
suburban places like la jolla or del mar because we live off a dirt
road that washes out every time it rains   so for us the rain is
really dramatic   though we hope for rains because by the end

of the summer all the chaparral has dried out from the endless
summer and were afraid of fire   but while we hope for rain we
hope it doesnt rain too much or all at once   because it often
comes down in torrents and our road gives out
          so i could understand how the salk center   a
marvelously designed modernist building in la jolla   could
contain some strange mistakes   it has a large courtyard whose
paving is marked by a grid of semicylindrical grooves that you
always trip on if youre not looking   and i used to wonder what
the grooves were for   they formed nice little squares in the
courtyard that rhymed with all the other square and rectangular
forms of the building   though that didnt explain why they
were so deeply incised that you tripped over them   but i
noticed that this rather blank central courtyard or piazza
overhung only by sky   swept dramatically westward to a
parapet that appeared to be overlooking the sea   but which
when you got there turned out somewhat anticlimatically   to
overlook a second little terrace with a dry fountain   below
which about a quarter of a mile of coastal scrub sloped gently
down to the beach   and i remembered reading somewhere that
the grooves were designed to feed rain water during the rainy
season into the fountain   where it would be continually
recycled eliminating the need for piped in water   so i wondered
why the fountain was dry   i wondered about a number of
other features of this remarkable building
          and one day i got into a conversation with one of
the workers who maintained the building   it was a friendly
conversation   so in the course of it i remarked that this was a
wonderfully designed building in which even the water needs
of the western fountain were accounted for in the form of the
building   or so i understood   by the design of the grooves in
the central plaza   that were calculated to pick up the rain

water that drained off the paving in the rainy season and carry it
   down to the pumps that would feed the fountain   within
which it would be continuously recirculated till the evaporation
   losses required it to be renewed from the plaza grooves during
the next rainy season   this was such an elegant system that
maintained the fountain in such a rational way with the constancy
   of nature that i wondered why the fountain was off
               it never worked   he said   and when i asked why not he
looked at me
               you know how often it rains in san diego he said?   how
often does it rain here
               not often this time of year
               you mean never this time of year he said   and this time
of year lasts seven eight months   and when the rains come it
rains a lot
               well   he said   somebody mustve figured the size of
   the grooves by the average rainfall   you know when it rains the
average rainfall?   never   so all the time it doesnt rain   the
   sand and dust that the wind blows around for seven eight
months collects in all the grooves   and when the unaverage
rain comes it overflows the grooves and carries all that sand and
   dust into the filter system and they have to pull the filters   it
never worked
               now i understood how this couldve happened how it
   almost had to happen   it couldnt have been helped   kahn
was an east coast architect with no experience but maybe a dream
   of california who had been dealing with another dreamer jonas
   salk   who was an east coast scientist who was a dreamer about
science and art and nature and even about what scientists did
   and he had informed his architect   out of his experience and
   out of his dream about what scientists could be expected to do
   to work in their laboratories of course but also to walk around in

the mild weather of lovely san diego and talk with other
scientists when they werent meditating in their studies
  overlooking the ocean about their work their ideas and dreams
    and when they were walking and talking and thinking together
  in the brilliant light of sunny southern california they might
want to write some of their ideas down and it would be nice to
have slates built into the walls of the building so they could write
  down some of their fresh ideas
        and accordingly the architect embedded slates in the walls
  of the building on which these reflective scientists could write
their freshest ideas down in the form of equations or shorthand
notes that they could then go back to their studies and meditate
  on before working them out in their laboratories
        yeah you can just imagine it   these guys letting anybody
  else in on an idea by chalking it out in public before they had a
  chance to publish or patent it or get a grant for it   that theyre
going to write something down that someone else could see
  before they could capitalize on it
        so there are slates out there that nobody uses and this is
  also part of the fantasy of designing something to accommodate
  activities that you desire and hope will occur in a building
  because youve designed the building to accommodate and
encourage them within its structure   and it accomodates many
  of these activities very well but there are others
        as a matter of fact jonas salk said to me one day that
  he was thinking of this courtyard as a place of art   maybe
having ann halperns dancers dancing in this courtyard
    and i looked at this grim stone courtyard which actually
  resembles nothing more closely than the terrace of curzio
malapartes castle   which figures so largely in godards movie
contempt   where it looks like some dreadful italian fascist fantasy
    and you think of halperns dancers who were dropping naked

out of trees in those days   and you imagine those lovely nude
bodies dropping off the landings of the staircases onto that
stone floor   its a terrible thought

and i said to jonas dont you think youd need padding
on the ground if she were to do her kind of dancing   dont
you think your terrace would affect nude bodies in a kind of
unpleasant way   and he walked away from me he was so
depressed   but ive had bad luck with jonas anyway   jonas is
one of those people who i think is a wonderful man   but i
kept offending him in unpredictable ways

id written an article on transient architecture in a local
magazine and i mentioned his building at one point   which
i described kind of playfully as a sort of mannerist modernist
mastodon   and having no light touch he thought that was
unfriendly   while i kind of like the building

but he has no light touch and he met me at another party
and he said to me   it seemed they they were always having
parties   apparently thats one of the things they used to do a
lot at the salk center   and they had this party and i was there
because back then i was the director of the unversity art gallery
and i was walking around holding a glass of chardonnay in my
hand   and jonas was again introduced to me   for the third
time   and he said to me young man he said   what have you
got against my building   and i tried to remember but i forgot
what id said   so i said its the the wrong shape   the wrong
shape he said   what shape should it be   i said it should have
been tall and cylindrical with a slot in the top for the coins   and
jonas stormed away pretty angry   though i imagine that jonas
probably didnt remember his childhood when old orthodox
jews with beards and earlocks used to come around in their long
coats and their fancy hats shaking blue and white cans in which
they collected coins for israel   so he may not have understood

my joke anyway   if he did i thought he wouldve laughed at it
but maybe not   because the joke may have touched on a central
point in the function of the building   because the building
 aside from its function of housing working scientists and their
laboratories has another function   as a letterhead
          the buildings character as a major work by what was
 surely one of americas most distinguished architects   is such
 that when youre an occupant of this building   a fellow of the
institute it houses youre that much likelier to get grants to
 support your work   though of course the people who become
 the occupants of the building   the fellows of the institute
 it houses   are the kind of people who bring grants to the
 building   so the tenants and the building are designed for each
other   the tenants are designed to bring grants to the building
 and the building is designed to bring grants to the tenants   and
 we know this because this is the form that science has taken in
america since the end of the second world war   so that we can
 say without a terrible amount of exaggeration that the greatest
 scientific discovery of the second part of the twentieth century
was the government grant   in the twenty first it may turn out to
 be the corporate partnership
          and of course the people who evaluate a scientists
 achievements often evaluate them in terms of the grants he or
she has gotten   in the universities and institutes in which
 science is mostly lodged theyll often consider whether to
promote this or that scientist by the size of his grants how much
 money hes made   and of course you cant continue to maintain
 the large laboratories purchase and keep up the expensive
 equipment that requires all that care and feeding   and employ
all those highly skilled people who help you do the kind of work
 that will get you your very next grant that will help you continue
 the kind of work in which almost all contemporary scientists are

invested   and most of these scientists are in competition with each other for the very large but limited amount of money   available in such grants   so all these considerations are part of the function of this building and enter into its structure

but in my case i didnt have such a problem   i wanted a place that could accommodate our human activity   and some of it was not too accommodatable in the space we had available   for one thing we found ourselves mainly living in the kitchen   the kitchen and dining room seem to be places where we do most of our living   the kitchen and dining room are so closely connected theyre really one large airy room walled on two sides with windows   and we have a huge table in the dining room   everybody likes to sit around so nobody goes into the living room because its dark and small

we have a living room that i think of mainly as a corridor between the kitchen dining room and the larger bedroom   its main use is as a corridor   and everybody uses it as a corridor on the way to the bathroom   or to our workrooms   its got a fireplace and dark wood panelled walls   so its kind of cozy a dark little den in the wintertime   if you have a fire going in the fireplace and if you keep the curtains drawn over the glass wall and doors   but if anyone opens the doors the rain comes in with them   once you open the door the rain pours in   so we almost never open the doors in the winter   and in the summer you want to open the curtains and doors to let in the air and the light   but you still have to keep the curtains drawn because the room gets too hot from the afternoon sun and the air never moves because it only comes in through the doors   so nobody really wants to spend time there except now and then on a winter night with a fire going   and now that we got a terrific wood stove for the dining room and kitchen everybodys happy because now we can close the door to the living room and

sit around the dining room table in the winter even when the
weather gets wet because theres no other heating in this old
california house

so we contribute mildy to the pollution of the
atmosphere   but so does most living   we use the dining
room and kitchen for most of our social living and we have the
bedroom for sleeping and two workrooms for working and
the living room for reading at night or listening to the stereo or
playing a video   so we have these usages

but what if we decided to design the house ourselves
what if we decided to design a house to house our usages
how would we do it   what kind of structure would it have
if we decided to do it   it would take time   time is a large
part of it   ive noticed this   one of the problems of life is that
it has a structure too   and its structure is a threatening
structure   its a transient state   you appear into it and
disappear from it   and each day carries the threat that the next
day may not come that is i assume one of the functions of
nightfall is to let you know that you may not see the next day

i think this is what happens when you see twilight   a certain
anxiety comes over people at twilight   certainly it comes over
me   more so now   but maybe it always did   people get
depressed at certain times of the day   i know my faculties start
to fade in the later afternoon   which you see is not normally
the highest point in my day   but of course im dislocated right
now and in a different time zone   it says four thirteen on my
watch but its really only one fourteen in my soul   and so im
still in california here in maryland   because if this were really
four fourteen in my body id really be struggling   it would be
really hard for me   four fourteen is a terrible time for me to be
thinking in any meaningfully human way

now we as humans imagine day as having a two part
structure   divided between the light and the dark the day
and the night   and we often imagine them as opposing forces
contending   alternating advantage from solstice to solstice
     but regularly returning at the equinoxes of spring and fall to
an equal division between night and day   yet they have a totally
different relation to the structure of our life
          the appearance of the sun in the morning always has a
terrific effect on me   we dont have any shades and the sun
comes in and wakes us up in the morning   and the door we
open to let air in has glass panes and transmits the sunlight as
early as possible   it transmits the first rays of sunlight very
early on nonovercast days and when that happens i wake up and
i dont care   im delighted to wake up to the sun   on the
other hand when it starts to fade i get depressed and if im in a
room that admits the sunset i have no pleasure in it   i have
no pleasurable sense of *le crépuscule*   crepuscular things dont
get to me i look out at the sunset and i measure the degree of
pollution by how terrifically beautiful it is   the more brilliant it
is the more polluted the atmosphere and i probably cant see the
offshore island   which we havent been seeing for a number of
years   i guess the island must have disappeared around 1970
     when we first got here you could see the offshore island
     then it disappeared for a while and then reappeared   and
then it disappeared for good   which goes to show you how it
happens
          but i began to think   what do we do   how do we set
up the situation if we are going to do this   what is our life like
     can we interrupt the structure of our life   which is a
serious structure   can we interrupt the structure of our life and
interpose a time of planning for building   in other words
     in order to make our life better should we make it worse

this sounds like a paradox but its not   because its quite true
that if you take the time out to plan and build an improvement
to your life you will have an extended period of making your
life worse while youre planning and building to make it better
    because youll have to deal with contractors   youre going to
have to sit down and try to rearrange all the habits of your life
to make them fit around the actions of contractors   and before
that youll have to go out and find a contractor to sit down with
    or a friend who does that kind of building   but if it is a
friend   it has to be the kind of friend that youd be willing to
tolerate for the length of time youd have to deal with him
            now i had in mind a wonderful charming friend   a
professional slovak   who was a friendly engineer turned
contractor named robert   who has very different reasons for
constructing buildings than we have for having a building made
    and that could turn out to be a problem   that is   we need
a building for very different reasons than he has been trained to
make buildings for   i suppose contractors make buildings
something like the way i make talk pieces   no thats not really
true   it isnt true at all   contractors make buildings the way
theyre used to making buildings   the way theyre paid to make
buildings by developers   in a way that will cost them the least
effort and make the most money for them and their developer
    while more or less conforming to the desires most of the
people the developer sells them to have learned from the look
and feel of the buildings that developers have trained them to
    in this way maybe theyre very different from architect
constructions and maybe we need an architect designed building
        but for a while ive had a theory that basically all
architecturally designed constructions have one essential
function   to serve as a maquette for a photograph in an
architectural journal   and as i understand things   thats what

theyre trained to do   and if they get over this   and there are
certainly architects who fight against this part of their training
theyre still architects and these are the habits of architects
and the only indispensable property of an architect is a
certain amount of negotiable charm   thats what all successful
architects have in common   and what they do with it is to get
commissioned to produce buildings that have a negotiable charm
which they exhibit as photographs in architectural magazines
          now a negotiable charm is something you dont have to
live with   if you live with it its no longer subject to negotiation
its living and living is something else   some people have
charm in their lives   for example my wife is a charming person
to live with   she might not be charming in public all the time
but i find her charming most of the time   architects i often
find charming but i dont think i could live with their charm
i dont think i could live with it even during the period of time
that theyre building   i dont think i could do it   so i realize
ill never get such a building made   because i cant bear the
architect and i cant bear the building hed make for me
          id rather put up with the open and peculiarly shoddy
structure that ive got because i can make do with it   and for
just that reason im not going to build another building
          certainly not at this time   because i cant stand the effort it
would take to go through this process   which would change
my life
          now as i said this i wondered if this was the structure of
my life demanding its replication and extension   you know
i cant deal with change at all   is that life choosing to assert
its autonomy and defending itself from any sort of change
          the idea that my sense of self is such that i must maintain
it at all costs   well   theres something in that

i have an attraction to the way i get up in the morning and
all the things that i usually do   there could be circumstances
that would change my life rather radically or lead me to change
it   but im not thinking of them at this moment   and if im
not thinking of them why should i change it   for example   it
seems to me that the state of this country is extremely fragile
    extraordinarily fragile in spite of its banality and blandness
    blandness and banality seem to be the tone in which america
is presently living   on the other hand we have been surrounded
    at the peripheries of this blandness and banality with poverty
and the threat of disasters and catastrophes of all kinds   any
one of which could disrupt our smooth flowing system of
    exchanges and throw it into a panic that could invoke vast
translations of our situations into something else and i think i
    could accommodate   ive accommodated in my life many times
to different sorts of circumstances   i havent for the last five
months   for the last twenty years or so i havent accommodated
    to major earth shifting changes   but it seems to me if the
changes dont come why go looking for them   if youre not
    facing a chasm why jump over it   if a chasm opens in the land
you jump over it or you try   and if you dont   you fail
        ive seen this happen with other people   my mother
    my mother lived a life of great orderliness   on a very small
scale   she was a kind of ascetic a depressive ascetic   thats not
a psychological condition   its an ontological condition no
    matter what psychotherapists say   and what she did was to
strip her life of all its elements of pleasure and risk and narrow
its space to a very small cell in which she could live a ritually
    ordered existence with whatever amount of discomfort she
could accommodate herself to   that would at the same time
relieve her of the much greater discomfort of having to change
    it   and this was her life   i always thought it would have been

better for her to have been a catholic   because then she could
have gone to early mass and done the stations of her cross on her
knees and confessed to all the petty sins that she could imagine
having committed and lived conveniently within the structural
regularity of a life of penance that could have been imposed
upon her as an act of charity by an intelligent and intuitive priest
                now she was living alone in new york city in a dark little
apartment on ocean parkway in a part of brooklyn in which she
had lived nearly her entire adult life   and i was living in southern
california   so i would only see her from time to time when i
went back to the city   and i would speak with her occasionally
on the phone and we would have these distant conversations
     because she had no interest in my life and she had so
little life of her own that it was very hard for me to find any
  points of interest in it   so the relationship between us was as
impoverished as the rest of her life   but i would phone her
  fairly regularly because i wanted to make sure that she was all
right   and i would see her occasionally when i went east
                one time i was scheduled to do a performance at the
ontario art center in toronto and just before i left my mother
called and said i cant do it any more   and i said why not   she
said terrible things are happening   what kind of things i said
  and she said terrible things   so i knew this was a turning point
and i said maybe i should come out and see whats happening
     and she said come quick before they kill me   i said who?
     she said some of them next door down the the street   and
this didnt make too much sense to me   she lived in a decent
working class neighborhood in brooklyn on ocean parkway and
there wasnt a chance that her neighbors were going to kill her
     but from her sound on the phone it was clear that she felt
they were   and i knew i would have to go   so i arranged to
stop off in new york on the way back from toronto   and very

early in the morning after my performance i found myself
sitting glumly in the nearly empty toronto airport with nothing
to do and sharing the wait with the only other passenger for that
  early flight who turned out to be a nuclear engineer and we
struck up a conversation

          it was five o'clock in the morning and we were sitting
  there alone and he was complaining about his job   which was
to inspect nuclear plants   it was a lonely job in which he had to
travel around from nuclear plant to nuclear plant looking for
  defects   and he was telling me what i hate about this job is that
as soon as i come to a place nobody wants to eat lunch with me
because they look at me as the enemy   because they think im
  going to find something and cause trouble   and i dont want to
cause anyone trouble   but my job is to be a safety engineer and
my job is to look for trouble and sometimes its there   and they
  may try to cover it up because they dont want to get blamed

          now down in winston salem theres a plant i inspected
    and i couldnt find anything wrong with it   but the tobacco
fields up to two miles around are dying   and we know there has
to be a leak   we know theres a leak somewhere in the system
and we cant get hold of all of the records but we know theres
got to be a leak somewhere   in this job you do the best you can
    but you cant help feeling like youre betraying people   and
  theyre suspicious and constantly covering up   and that always
make me feel bad and i wish i could quit   but its my job   this
was our tired conversation at five o'clock in the morning as we
waited for our plane to new york   and i began wondering oh
  my god what nuclear plant is near us   theres one in san onofre
about forty miles away thats constantly being dismantled and
  remantled   but now he was no longer talking to himself but to
an outsider like me   and he gave me a very rational account of
why we shouldnt worry about the san onofre nuclear plant

58

even if there were problems   because there were lots of
safeguards and regular inspections and lots of inspectors like
him   and when it came to talking to outsiders like me he had
real faith in the reliability of science and he seemed to forget
about the tobacco fields around winston salem   i have faith in
science too i said   but i dont have faith in american contractors
i can have faith in science but i dont have faith in american
plumbing   you remember a few years ago they were putting
nuclear waste in cans that were supposed to stay sealed for a
thousand years   do you know anyone in america who can make
a can that could stay sealed for a thousand years
     so i was on my way down to see my mother and when i
got there i could see that the neighborhood had changed   itd
gotten a little poorer   there were black and brown kids in the
street playing cheerful games now   and all the buildings were
a little older and a little more run down   but otherwise the
neighborhood looked pretty much the same   except that my
mother has a kind of xenophobic relation to people of color
     so i could see why she thought terrible things were going to
happen   and she was also starting to sound confused   that
was also part of the structure of her life   or maybe she wasnt
really confused   maybe it was just that as her life continued to
contract within the four walls of her apartment   all she could
see were the images that got projected on the four walls of her
mind   maybe thats also part of the structure of a life   that as
it approaches its ending it contracts and withdraws into itself
     there are fewer interchanges with the outside world   and you
lose your defenses against your fears and youre thrown back on
your own mental resources and become more who youve always
been
     now i know that new york city has always been racist
in a complicated way   and almost all the people who come

from new york have a firm belief that color is a profound aspect of human character   and the degree to which most of my european relatives have internalized this belief is amazing   so maybe its a european fantasy   its as if the colors black and brown had some deep metaphorical significance for them that ive never really understood

but whatever the source of this feeling   there was my mother huddling terrified in her apartment surrounded by neighbors who looked to me like perfectly ordinary middle class black and latino people   so i made plans to move her out of her old neighborhood in brooklyn to pacific beach in san diego

but not before i was subjected to a very strange experience

for some reason i didnt understand shed begun to worry about her bank   a little bank next to the beverly theater on church avenue near mcdonald avenue that shed had her savings account in for years   it seemed shed come to believe the bank was cheating her out of her interest or not entering her interest regularly enough   so shed started cashing her social security checks at the bank and taking the cash back to her apartment where she got no interest at all   and where she was always afraid of being robbed   though shed never been robbed never known anyone whod been robbed and was probably more in danger of being robbed carrying her cash through the streets

and i never understood why she thought the bank was robbing her of her interest or how this could be prevented by taking her money home

but i guess when youve retreated within the walls of your mind its hard to pay attention to anything outside of your fears and your hopes   and because by now she had accumulated a fairly large amount of cash in her apartment she was now more afraid of being robbed in her apartment than being robbed of her interest by the bank and she wanted me to go with her to

take the cash back to the bank and make sure that she got her
  interest recorded properly   but before that she said we had to
  count the money that we were going to take to the bank   that
seemed sensible enough   and i agreed to it   but first she had
  to get the money out of the place where she was keeping it safe
  in the plumbing

        when i say it was in the plumbing i mean it was inside the
porcelain washbasin   so i watched her go into the bathroom
  take a loose porcelain tile out of the back of the washbasin
stand   reach in and pull out what looked like a plastic bag from
between the water pipes   inside this plastic bag was another
  plastic bag that looked something like a tobacco pouch closed
with lots of rubber bands   and inside that was an envelope
  stuffed with money   and there it was   three thousand single
dollar bills stored between the leaking pipes in her washstand
    and i had to help her count it

        now counting three thousand single dollar bills is a
  strange experience   its a little bit like david tudor separating
spices that have gotten mixed up together on the floor   and i go
  through it   one two three four   i counted it three times and
  each time i got a different number   different by about two
dollars   and my mother wanted me to count it again   but i
  said no   forget it   ill give you the two dollars   im not going
to count it again   then we took it to the bank   but there was a
  black teller at the bank   who was very patient when my mother
  gave him the money and made him count it over again   and he
was still patient when she went over her interest and made
  him check to see if it was really entered correctly   and she was
  about to start arguing with him about it when i grabbed her arm
and hustled her out of there   so we had come to an abrupt turn
  in the structure of her life

and i moved her to southern california   which was a
little bit like hamlet getting shipped off to england where they
were all crazy and no one would notice   and no one would have
noticed her because i moved her into a sunny little apartment in
pacific beach where she could be as independent as she wanted
  and i could still keep an eye on her and all the bank tellers were
white   but this situation didnt last too long   because in spite
of the fact that i took care of her rent and all of her bills   she
still had her bank book and her bank account   and she would
go into her local bank branch on garnet two three times a day
and demand that the tellers enter the interest into her passbook
    and i got the impression that all of the tellers would scramble
for the restroom or their coffee break at the sight of an elderly
lady in an orange hat holding a passbook in her hand
        but this was a situation that didnt last too long   things
started going really bad at her apartment in a way i hadnt
  expected   i had moved her into this sunny little apartment
complex on la playa   partly because of its manager   a
paternalistic ex-navy man with a soft spot for elderly ladies
    occasionally he would drive her to the shopping center on
garnet so she could get her groceries   and from time to time
he would look in on her to see if she was all right   and he was
even a bit of a pain in the ass about it   because he would call
  me whenever he thought she wasnt   and this happened a bit
too often   so i was really surprised when my mother began
to complain about him   how can you complain about him i
asked her when he even takes you shopping   thats because hes
  interested in my money she said hes always talking about my
  money   whenever i say i cant afford something because its too
expensive he says go on youre a rich lady   youve got a son
  whos a professor   you can afford it   one time i caught him
sneaking into my apartment when i wasnt there and when i asked

him what he was doing he said he was fixing the light switch
so? what do you think he was doing?
he was stealing things
what kind of things?
my ice cube trays
i realized things were getting very bad and the time had come to move her out of there   so i found her a place in a home for active elderlies   which meant they got their rooms cleaned their meals prepared and ate in a common dining room
but they came and went freely as they felt like   a few of them even had cars but mostly they had group activities and got taken to the shopping on a fairly regular schedule in the company shuttle when the residents could remember it   and if they mostly couldnt a staff member rounded them up and reminded them
i had gotten her into this place called collwood villa and it seemed perfectly adequate   this was another stage in the structure of her life and i thought i understood it
theres a traditional image that divides a human life into stages   you begin as a child and youre dependent on the tall people leaning over you for your survival and nearly everything else   except your perceptions   but as you grow your perceptions begin to outstrip your competences   you see what other people do and imagine that you can do them too   and sometimes you can and sometimes you cant   but you begin to find that the people leaning over and holding you up are holding you back   and theyre beginning to bother you   because youre convinced you can stand on your own   and maybe you can and maybe you cant but you dont want them hanging over you anyway   and after a while they let go   and you do the things you can and the things you cant as well as you can   and youre on your own   over this period of time that youre a fairly

competent person and you never thought about what happens at
its end

 but even before that   after a while   small
incompetences begin to appear   maybe you cant run a five
 minute mile any more   or maybe you can   but you step in a
pothole while running on the beach and twist your ankle and it
takes a couple of weeks instead of a couple of days to heal
 but whatever they are theyre   small signals of a kind of
decline   and you deal with these signals in a complicated way
 you dont really adjust to them psychologically   because
 theyre mostly little things that you cant do any more   so you
adjust to them without taking much notice   like i cant stay
up all night at a party any more talking and drinking and get up
 fresh the next morning at six the way i could when i was a kid
so i go to sleep around twelve and tell myself ive become
a morning person because the sun comes in my window and
wakes me up at six   but after a while there are a lot of these
little signals   a lot of these small incompetences pile up and i
 imagine theres going to come a time when i cant do even more
 things   i see it foretold in the life of my relatives facing a
declining day   its like going to my window and looking at the
sunset

 i dont like looking at the sunset you know   its not
 beautiful   its an intimation of an ending   a structural effect
that points to closure like the door of a house   and it happened
with my mother   i got a call from the residential hotel for
active elderlies   they called and told me i would have to do
 something   and when i asked what was the matter they were
very delicate about it   they thought she would be better off in a
different kind of place with more care   she couldnt manage
 at collwood any longer   and when i asked what it was that she
 couldnt manage any more that shed been able to manage up to

then   they simply said i would have come and see for myself
  so i drove down there and it was an understatement
          whatever my mother was doing forgetting things there
  was one thing she wasnt forgetting   and that was to take very
good care of her fecal materials   i remember coming into her
  room and it had a weirdly rank odor   the musky smell of
  decaying matter   coming from a chest of drawers from the
  closet from under the night table   i opened a drawer i opened a
drawer and saw it   a small column shaped like a little snowman
  a foul smelling greyish micromonument perhaps four inches high
      and there were many more of them in various shapes and
  sizes secreted away in a drawer in a closet in a pair of shoes
      except in the one place you might have expected them   in
  the bathroom   where the toilet was stuffed up with entire rolls
of toilet paper   i suppose something had gone wrong with the
  toilet mechanism   maybe it had gotten somewhat clogged so
that it didnt flush right and overflowed and shed tried to fix it by
plugging it up with toilet paper   which only made things
  worse   made the water spill out onto the floor so she couldnt
use the toilet any more   so she had to take care of her shit in a
different way hiding it carefully all about the room   but she has
  no memory of ever doing this
          she knows terrible things have been happening in her
  room and thinks people come in when shes sleeping and do
  disgusting things but she doesnt know what they are because
she forgets   so maybe none of this is true   maybe people have
been taking things from her   shes been losing things all her life
      when she was a little girl she lost her mother   they sent
  her away to stay with her grandmother when her mother was
pregnant with her next child and she woke up in the night
  walking in her sleep searching for her mothers warmth opened
  her arms and embraced a stove   she lost a husband after three

years of marriage   he died of a strep throat or medical
incompetence   lost a second she walked out on who died of
cancer   lost a stepdaughter she abandoned to her exhusbands
relatives and a son who moved out as soon as he was sixteen
     and now she was losing pieces of herself   the names of her
sisters her mothers face even her own shit   it was all going
away   so she stuffed up the toilet and began saving her
excrement and hiding it in secret places   moulding it into little
monuments of loss
          so i realize its time to get her out of there and i start
looking for a different place   i knew there must be some
structure to the way people care for the elderly in humane ways
     you hope for this   weve heard of eskimo societies where
when people start stuffing up the toilet they put them on ice
floes and they raise their voices and sing oh how happy we are
     how happy we are to be on this ice floe floating away   but
we dont have ice floes and we have a different system   what
we do in a very humane way is to find them elysian fields called
nursing homes   and in these pleasant places they wander
around slightly dazed or bananas having friendly conversations
with themselves   and i went around to a number of these
places looking for a place for my mother   and the first of
these places i came to   all of the residents were in wheelchairs
and i asked how come all of these people are in wheelchairs
     i know they cant think but why cant they walk   they said its
to protect them from falling   they dont always know where
they are and sometimes they fall   but surely they dont all fall
why dont you wait till they fall?   and it turned out it was a
matter of insurance   it costs too much to insure them against
falling   so whether they would fall or not it was cheaper to
keep them in wheelchairs and make sure they didnt fall

but i finally found a place where some of the residents
at least were walking around   in a daze to be sure   but some
of them were talking and smiling and some of them were even
  singing and one little old lady came up to me and said "auf die
strasse"   a phrase that she repeated as if she wanted some kind
  of answer   so i said "wo wohin"   but she simply repeated
the one phrase over and over again   "auf die strasse auf die
strasse"   and i realized there were no streets here   this was
  a postmodern suburban nursing home located on the avenue of
industry between a software company and a biotech outfit in
bland desolate east san diego   so i explained to her in german
  that there were no streets here in this part of san diego but
there was a garden and she might like to go out into the garden
    but she merely repeated the same phrase over and over again
    "auf die strasse auf die strasse"
        so i realized that this was the right place for my mother
    the people were not unhappy here   they were taken good
  care of   they could wander up and down the hallways freely
silently or talking to themselves or they could go out into the
garden   because by this time my mother didnt recognize me any
more when i came to see her   she would smile when she saw
me and say you look like a nice man   who are you?   and i
would say im your son david   and she would say oh im so glad
    but is it really you   and the conversations would go like that
as long as she was still able to talk   and then sometimes she
would start to pray   in hebrew   now my mother was never
religious and didnt know hebrew   but some rabbinical visitor
  to the nursing home told them something about hebrew prayers
and prayed with them   and she remembered this prayer or at
least its beginning which went   *shma yisroel adonoi eloheynu adenoi*
  ekhod   which means something to the effect that blessed is this
guy whose day of rest has lasted these past five thousand plus

years because he is the one and only lord of israel and
everybody else and hes why you are where you are and doing
what youre doing and not doing what youre not doing
          but she says this and smiles in the same sweet way she
does when she talks to anyone who comes by whether theyre
listening or not   so my mother has now become a performer in
a performance that is indeterminate in respect of its context
     and she wanders around in this environment cheerfully
enough   as you might imagine someone might who had devoted
a large part of her life to removing things from it that might
have provided it with problems or interest
          now how could i describe the structure of this life   is
there a structure to her life in my sense   there may be such a
structure but i dont know if it really means a lot   i can look
at her beginnings through what ive heard from her and others
who knew her and i can look at her ending   so i can imagine a
partially continuous curve   i say partially because there are
parts i dont know   places where the curve breaks down
     and also because i can imagine that lives are not completely
continuous   consciousness doesnt seem to be continuous
     her consciousness certainly   she cant really connect between
her now and her earlier states   shes forgotten her father and
her mother and sisters and brothers and she doesnt know who i
am   though she will remember little bits   so its partially
continuous   and during these little periods of continuity
there are regularities recurrences of a sort   comings and goings
waking and sleeping night and day   openings and closings
     and these mean different things   openings and closings
are not equivalent   beginnings and endings are not the same
     there is something in the nature of endings that is not at all
like a beginning   no matter how open you make them   and if
i make an ending that is very open   if i were to quit talking at

this very moment   which i could do   as the presence of my
tape recorder suggests
                            but i wont do it   not for that reason
    not just to create a kind of arbitrary openness
                                                    because my
    sense is that while here are many kinds of closures   closure is
an inevitability of anything you can identify as an act a
performance or even a process   because the tendency of a
process is to play itself out in a certain direction and either to
    arrive at an ending or imply one as you walk away from it   so
even if you walk away from it   it still feels closed
                now this connects with something jackson maclow
    mentioned to me that a poet he knew had said that one of the
problems with my talks is that they have a tendency to close on
grand stories that function like the final couplet of a sonnet
    which i thought was an amusing idea   but what occurred
to me now was that whats different in the works i do and find
interesting
                    and i rarely find sonnets interesting   is not so much
    the manner of ending but the scale   magnitude seems to have
a lot to do with structure   a work of great magnitude cant have
a lot in common with a work that is easily encompassed in a
    much smaller scale   theres something fundamentally different
which seems as if it shouldnt be   but there is   so that when
you close a very long work   or when a very long life comes to
    an end   as my mothers is coming to an end   she's 86 now
    or my father in laws   which has been a much more brilliant
    and attractive life   hes a poet and a painter and hes also losing
his faculties but its different   lets say he were to be faced with a
    dreadful ending somewhat similar to my mothers   how much
    would the ending count   how much would his ending count in
the meaning of his life

if you think about it   the ending seems to count in my
mothers case maybe because thats what ive told you about   or
maybe its really meaningful and rhymes with the rest of her life
    so that its a last couplet of deprivation so to speak   but im
not sure thats so   it may be only that this sudden shrinking of
her life shook me up and was meaningful to me   in effect
who remembers how crime and punishment ends?   i certainly
cant   i remember the beginning and the middle   i remember
moving in the direction of an ending   toward closure   but i
dont remember the ending   i dont remember the ending of any
dostoyevsky novel ive ever read   i dont remember the ending
of don quixote   and whats interesting i dont even remember
the ending of ulysses
    i know theres mollie bloom and all those yeses   but i
dont remember it as an ending   her long daydream seems to
be going on all the time either simultaneously with or overlapping
all the other parts of the novel   and it doesnt seem to function
as an ending for that comic and violent work   which doesnt
really have an ending   but what if joyce had intended to
produce mollie blooms erotic daydream as a lyrical ending like an
absurd mozartian allegro wrapping up a dark symphony   would
that make it a significant part of its structure
    not for me   so in this sense structural issues seem to be
somewhat different from what i thought they were   i believe
there are serious issues of structure but theyre not based simply
on the obvious facts of disposition or configuration   and
thats because there is a certain subjectivity in this   not my
subjectivity or your subjectivity but a kind of generalized
subjectivity that calls it into existence
    now i think structure depends on the existence of a
particular experiencing subject for which it manifests itself and
which it may even call into existence   in a sense the structure
creates the subjectivity for which it exists   and in this sense its

70

only immanent   so the structure of a human life as it presents
itself to itself is not something we can directly observe   we can
only discern it by inference   in this way its like the works that
 we make
             we imagine i imagine as i work certain kinds of shapes
 i feel im creating   and i know they may not be experienced by
anybody else   and i dont care   but seeing them take shape
provides me with a way to go on   and helps me get to end
    not to closure   but to get through with my work   and this
 particular way in which ive been working today   in building
this piece there was a certain central structural issue for me
    how do i build something that takes an articulate shape yet
resists closure while everything else in me wishes to close it on a
formal note   so i wont do it

        these pieces were performed in 1989   four years later
        we found our charming architect and an artist contractor
        we rebuilt our house and my mother died

David Antin is Professor Emeritus of Visual Arts at the University of California, San Diego. Among his most recent books are *i never knew what time it was* (2005), *A Conversation with David Antin* (2002), *what it means to be avant-garde* (1993), and *Selected Poems: 1963-1973* (1991).

Kenneth Goldsmith is author of eight books of poetry, founding editor of the online archive UbuWeb (ubu.com), and the editor *I'll Be Your Mirror: The Selected Andy Warhol Interviews*. He teaches writing at The University of Pennsylvania, where he is a senior editor of PennSound, a online poetry archive.

Singing Horse Press Titles

Charles Alexander, *Near Or Random Acts*. 2004, $15
Julia Blumenreich, *Meeting Tessie*. 1994, $6.00
Linh Dinh, *Drunkard Boxing*. 1998, $6.00
Norman Fischer, *Success*. 1999, $14.00
Norman Fischer, *I Was Blown Back*. 2005, $15.00
Phillip Foss, *The Ideation*. 2004, $15.00
Eli Goldblatt, *Without a Trace*. 2001, $12.50
Mary Rising Higgins, *)cliff TIDES((*. 2005, $15.00
Karen Kelley, *Her Angel*. 1992, $7.50
Kevin Killian & Leslie Scalapino, *Stone Marmalade*. 1996, $9.50
Hank Lazer, *The New Spirit*. 2005, $14.00
McCreary, Chris & Jenn, *The Effacements / a doctrine of signatures*. 2002, $12.50
David Miller, *The Waters of Marah*. 2002, $12.50
Andrew Mossin, *Epochal Body*. 2004, $15.00
Harryette Mullen, *Muse & Drudge*. 1995, $12.50
Harryette Mullen, *S*PeRM**K*T*. 1992, $8.00
Paul Naylor, *Playing Well With Others*. 2004, $15.00
Gil Ott, *Pact*. 2002, $14.00
Heather Thomas, *Practicing Amnesia*. 2000, $12.50
Rosmarie Waldrop, *Split Infinities*. 1998, $14.00
Lewis Warsh, *Touch of the Whip*. 2001, $14.00

These titles are available online at **www.singinghorsepress.com**, or through Small Press Distribution, at (800) 869-7553, or online at **www.spdbooks.org**.